Manual P
First Edition

PSYCHROMETRICS:
THEORY & APPLICATION

Air Conditioning Contractors of America

2800 Shirlington Road, Suite 300
Arlington, VA 22206

Acknowledgements
Manual P
First Edition

This Manual was prepared by the
Air Conditioning Contractors of America

Author:

Hank Rutkowski, P.E.
ACCA Technical Director

Review and Technical Assistance:

Rod Beever
Product Manager, Borg-Warner Environmental Systems, Inc.,
(York, PA)

Don Cochell
Technical Advisor, Detroit Edison
(Detroit, MI)

R. Lee Culpepper
Program Manager, Tennessee Vallee Authority
(Chattanooga, TN)

Stephen D. Kennedy
Southern Company Services
(Atlanta, GA)

Nance Lovvorn
Technical Advisor, Alabama Power Company
(Birmingham, AL)

Thomas McGarry
Residential Marketing, Training Director
Rochester Gas & Electric (Rochester, NY)

Barney Menditch, P.E.
President of General Heating Engineering Co., Inc.
(Capitol Heights, MD)

Earl Nichols
MS Power Company
(Gulfport, MS)

Alfred A. Piff
President of A/C Contracting Company, Inc.
(Mobile, AL)

Ron Yingling
NAHB Research Foundation
(Rockville, MD)

TABLE OF CONTENTS

LIST OF FIGURES

OVERVIEW OF PSYCHROMETRICS MANUAL

Understanding and Reading the Psychrometric Chart

The Psychrometric Chart is a convenient and concise summary of the properties of air. These properties include (or are related to) temperature, moisture content, heat content and density.

Section 1 itemizes the various properties of air and shows how these properties are represented by the lines that make up the psychrometric chart. This section also illustrates how a single point on the psychrometric chart provides information on seven properties of air.

Psychrometric Processes and Calculations

Section 2 discusses how the psychrometric chart can be used to provide a graphic representation of the change produced in the properties of air when it is processed by HVAC equipment.

Points on the chart can be used to quantify the properties of air at the beginning and end of a process. The process itself can be represented by a line which connects these points. Equations can be used to establish the relationship between the change in one or more air properties and the capacity of the HVAC equipment.

Room Sensible Heat Ratio and Room CFM

Section 3 includes discussion about room (or zone) design dry bulb temperature and relative humidity and how it will be maintained by the cooling equipment. This section defines the room sensible heat ratio line and how to maintain design conditions within the room or zone.

Coil Sensible Heat Ratio

Section 4 discusses the conditions needed to maintain the indoor design dry bulb temperature and relative humidity. This section defines the coil sensible heat ratio line and the equation needed to arrive at the only possible supply air condition.

Psychrometrics of HVAC Systems

Section 5 illustrates how the psychrometric chart can be used to analyze the particular processes associated with the various types of heating and cooling systems. This analysis will help the designer understand the advantages and disadvantages of various types of HVAC systems.

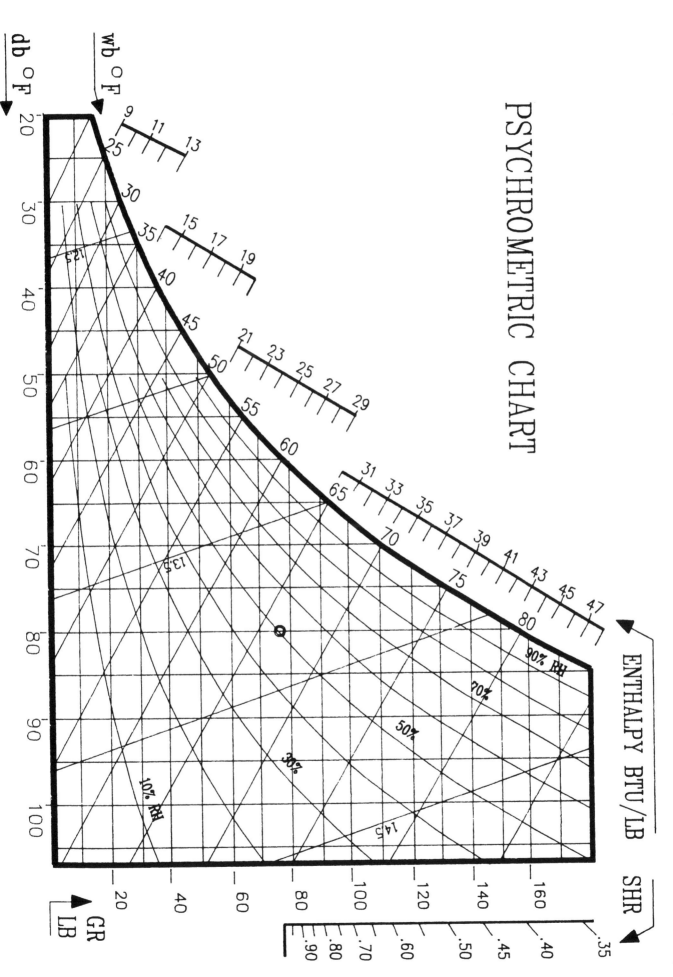

PSYCHROMETRIC CHART

7

Section 1
Understanding and Reading the Psychrometric Chart

The psychrometric chart is a useful and time-saving design tool. The chart describes all of the possible combinations of temperature, moisture content, density and heat content properties that can occur in the air we breathe. The chart can also be used to make calculations to determine the sensible and latent loads associated with HVAC equipment processes (i.e., heating, sensible cooling, mixing air streams, humidification or dehumidification). It can be used to predict whether people will find a given indoor temperature and humidity condition to be comfortable or uncomfortable, or if condensation will occur on a surface such as a wall or pane of glass (dew point), or if enthalpy control is cost effective.

At first glance, the various lines on the psychrometric chart are somewhat intimidating. Actually, only six different lines are required to completely describe the physical properties (condition point) of the air. The discussion that follows will identify each property and the corresponding line on the chart which represents that property.

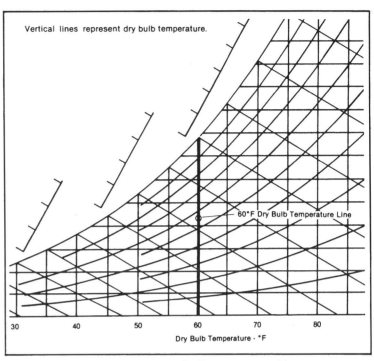

Figure 1.1 Dry Bulb Temperature Line

Dry Bulb Temperature
Vertical lines on the psychrometric chart represent dry bulb temperature. This temperature is the temperature measured by an ordinary thermometer. For example, the vertical line shown in Figure 1.1 represents a dry bulb temperature of 60°F.

Specific Humidity
On the psychrometric chart, horizontal lines represent specific humidity. Specific humidity is the amount of water (by weight) in each pound of air. In the example shown in Figure 1.2 (on the following page), the specific humidity is 0.010 pounds of water per pound of air or 70 grains of water per pound of air.

Note that the specific humidity can either be expressed in pounds of water per pounds of dry air, or grains of water per pound of dry air. Note that the pounds of water that can be absorbed by a pound of air is a fairly small number (.001 to .025). It is more convenient to use "grains" to describe the specific humidity of air. (When "grain" units are used, the numbers which describe the specific humidity of the air range from about 10 to about 170.) To convert one set of units to another set of units, remember that there are 7005 grains of water in one pound of water. Figure 1.3 (on the following page) illustrates this relationship.

Note: Specific humidity will be expressed in GRAINS/LB throughout the remainder of this manual.

Wet Bulb Temperature
Lines which slant from the lower right hand corner of the chart toward the upper left hand corner represent two different properties. These lines can either represent wet bulb temperature or enthalpy. (This is not exactly correct, but for practical purposes, wet bulb lines are shown as being coincident with enthalpy lines.)

Wet bulb temperature is measured by an ordinary dry bulb thermometer which has wet gauze wrapped around its bulb and air blowing across it at 50 FPM. During this measurement, the water in the gauze evaporates as it absorbs heat from the fluid contained in the thermometer bulb. This causes the wet bulb thermometer to indicate a temperature which is lower than the corresponding dry bulb reading. The rate of evaporation of the moisture from the wet gauze is directly related to the dryness of the surrounding air.

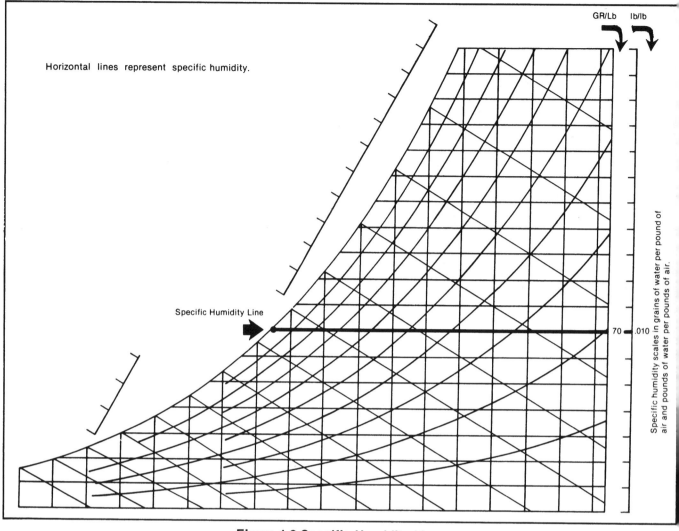

Horizontal lines represent specific humidity.

Specific Humidity Line

Specific humidity scales in grains of water per pound of air and pounds of water per pounds of air.

GR/Lb   lb/lb

70   .010

Figure 1.2 Specific Humidity Line

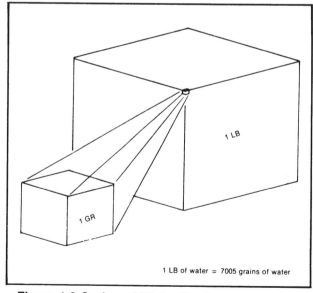

1 LB

1 GR

1 LB of water = 7005 grains of water

Figure 1.3 Grains of Water Per Pound of Water

Wet bulb readings will be lower for dry air than they will be for humid air. Thus, the difference between the wet bulb temperature and the dry bulb temperature is related to the moisture content (humidity) of the surrounding air.

Figure 1.4 shows that the wet bulb temperature of the air is 60°F and the dry bulb temperature of the air is 70°F. This indicates that the air has a specific humidity of 62 grains per pound.

Figure 1.4 Wet Bulb Temperature Line
When air becomes completely saturated with water, it cannot absorb additional moisture and the water contained in the gauze cannot evaporate. When this occurs, the wet bulb thermometer will read the same temperature as the dry bulb thermometer. Coincident wet and dry bulb temperatures always fall on the saturation line. The saturation line represents air that contains all the water it can possibly hold and coresponds to the 100 percent relative humidity condition. However, if the wet bulb temperature of the air is less than the dry bulb temperature of the air, the air will only be partly saturated. Figure 1.5 shows that if the wet bulb temperature of the air is 60°F and the dry bulb temperature of the air is 60°F, the air is completely saturated (100% R.H.) and has a specific humidity of 78 grains per pound.

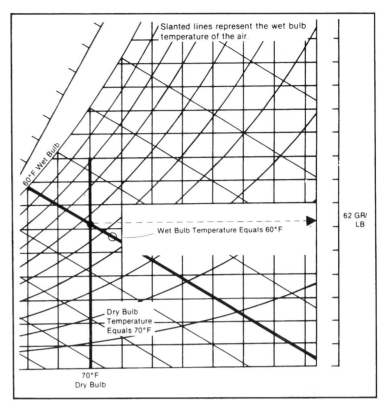

Figure 1.4 Wet Bulb Temperature Line

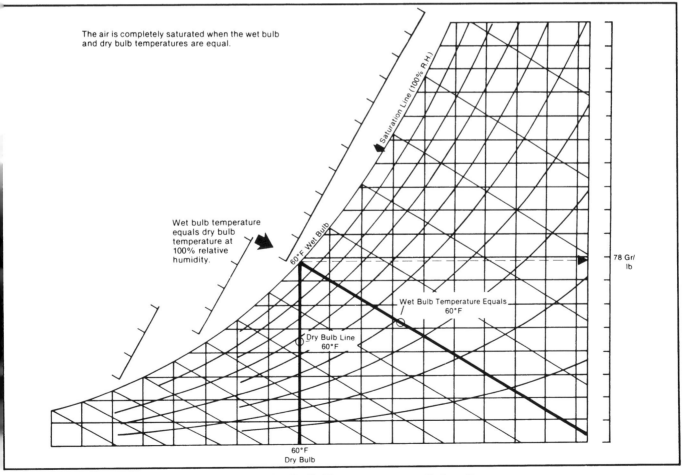

Figure 1.5 Wet Bulb Temperature at Saturation

Relative Humidity

The curved lines on the chart represent relative humidity. Relative humidity is an indication of the degree of saturation of the air. Air that is completely saturated has a relative humidity of 100%. Perfectly dry air has a relative humidity of 0%. Most of the time, air has a relative humidity that falls between these two extremes.

Figure 1.6 shows the heavy dark line which indicates the possible conditions when the relative humidity of the air is equal to 50%.

What is the difference between relative humidity and specific humidity? Relative humidity only indicates how close the air is to being saturated, but it does not provide any information on how much water (grains) is actually in a pound of air. In Figure 1.7, you can see that air which has 50% relative humidity can have many different specific humidities such as 60 GR/LB or 110 GR/LB.

Specific humidity indicates exactly how much water each pound of air holds, but does not indicate the degree of saturation. (Specific humidity is often called "absolute humidity".) In this manual, "specific humidity" will be used exclusively but the two terms are interchangeable. In the example shown by Figure 1.8, air which has a specific humidity of 80 GR/LB can have many different relative humidities such as 40%, 65% or 80%.

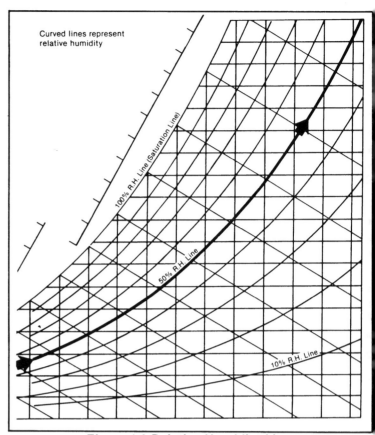

Figure 1.6 Relative Humidity Line

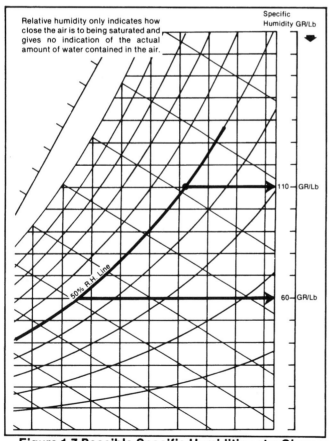

Figure 1.7 Possible Specific Humidities at a Given Relative Humidity

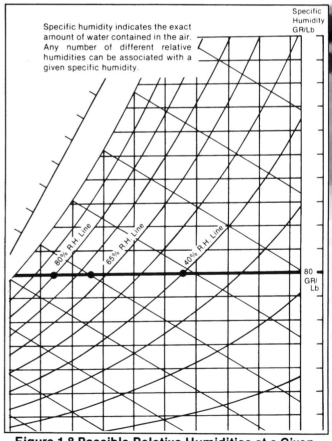

Figure 1.8 Possible Relative Humidities at a Given Specific Humidity

12

Dew Point

The dew point of air at any given condition corresponds to the dry bulb (or wet bulb) temperature at which air becomes completely saturated (100 percent relative humidity). The dew point is reached as the dry bulb temperature is reduced and the specific humidity is held constant.

In the example shown by Figure 1.9, air which has a dry bulb temperature of 75°F and a relative humidity of 60% has a dew point of 60°F.

Enthalpy

As noted previously, lines which slant from the lower right hand corner of the chart toward the upper left hand corner can represent either enthalpy lines or wet bulb temperature lines.

Enthalpy is the amount of heat (sensible and latent) contained in the air. This heat is expressed in BTU of heat per pound of air. The example in Figure 1.10 shows each pound of air holds 30 BTU of heat.

Specific Volume

Lines which slant steeply from the lower right hand corner of the chart toward the upper left hand corner represent specific volume lines. Specific volume is the volume (in cubic feet) that one pound of air occupies. In heating and cooling work, the specific volume varies between 12 and 15 cu-ft/lb (air). Note that the units used for specific volume are cu-ft/lb and that these units are the reciprocal of the density (lb/cu-ft) of the air. In the example shown by Figure 1.11, the specific volume line indicates that each pound of air occupies 14 cubic feet.

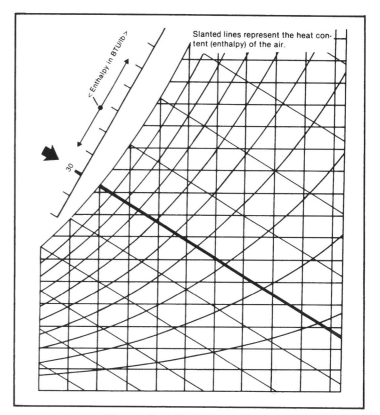

Figure 1.10 Enthalpy Line

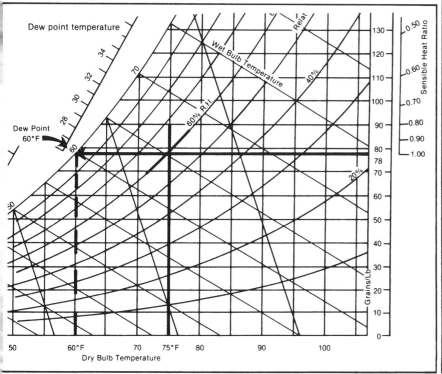

Figure 1.9 Dew Point Condition

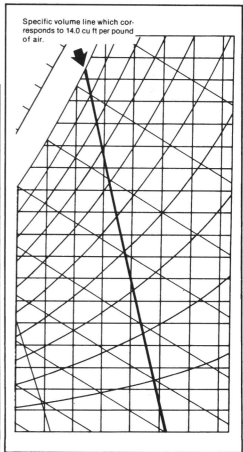

Figure 1.11 Specific Volume Line

13

Figure 1.12 summarizes the various properties of air and the corresponding lines drawn on the psychrometric chart that represent these properties.

Figure 1.13 summarizes the property lines for air at a specific condition.

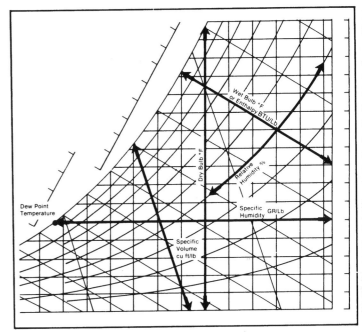

Figure 1.12 General Summary Properties and Property Lines

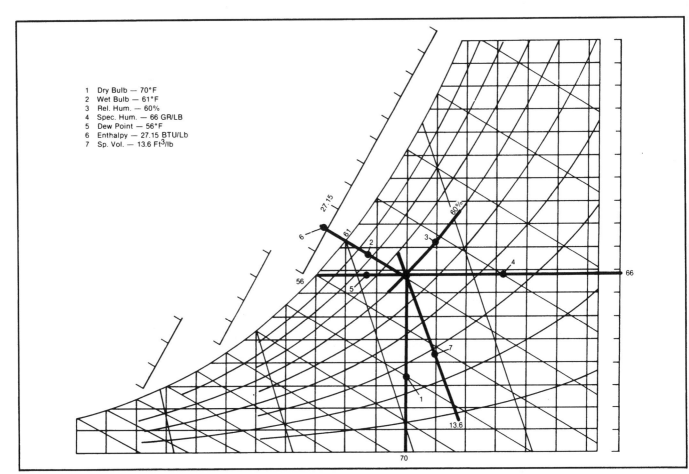

1 Dry Bulb — 70°F
2 Wet Bulb — 61°F
3 Rel. Hum. — 60%
4 Spec. Hum. — 66 GR/LB
5 Dew Point — 56°F
6 Enthalpy — 27.15 BTU/Lb
7 Sp. Vol. — 13.6 Ft^3/lb

Figure 1.13 Summary of Properties for Air at a Specific Condition

Examples

Now that the lines on the chart are identified, the significance of a point on the chart is apparent. A single point on the chart can represent any or all of the properties previously described. Note that the intersection of any two property lines will locate a point on the chart and the other four properties can be readily determined once the point which corresponds to these two properties is located. The following examples indicate the procedure.

Example 1.1

Given: db = 70°F   wb = 65°F

Figure 1.14 Indicates That:
Specific Humidity = 84.5 GR/LB
Relative Humidity = 78%
Enthalpy = 30 BTU/LB
Specific Volume = 13.6 CU. FT./LB
Dew Point = 62°F

Example 1.2

Given: db = 85   RH = 30%

Figure 1.15 Indicates That:
Wet Bulb = 63.6°F
Specific Humidity = 53.5 GR/LB
Enthalpy = 28.8 BTU/LB
Specific Volume = 13.9 CU. FT./LB
Dew Point = 50°F

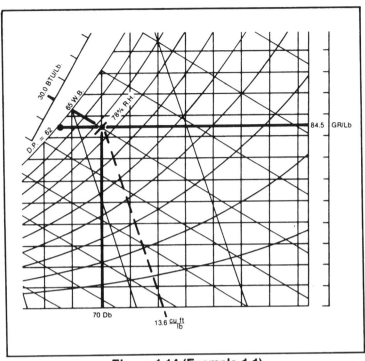

Figure 1.14 (Example 1.1)

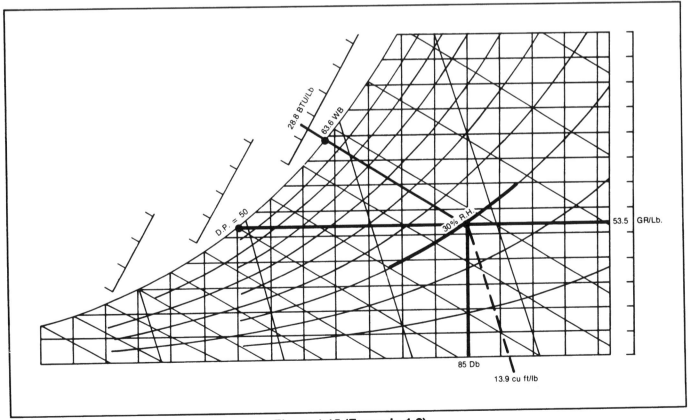

Figure 1.15 (Example 1.2)

15

Practice Problems — Section 1

1.1 Given: Enthalpy = 25.0 BTU/Lb and DB = 70°F

    Find: wb =
                RH =
                Specific Volume =
                Specific Humidity =
                Dew Point =

1.2 Given: Specific Humidity = 100 GR/Lb and wb = 75°F

    Find: db =
                RH =
                Specific Volume =
                Enthalpy =
                Dew Point =

1.3 Given: db = 60°F and wb = 60°F

    Find: RH =
                Specific Volume =
                Enthalpy =
                Specific Humidity =
                Dew Point =

Check your work. Refer to the solutions which are provided at the back of this manual.

Section 2
Psychrometric Processes and Calculations

The previous section explained how a point on the chart completely describes the condition (properties) of air. Because heating and cooling equipment can change some (or all) of the properties of the air, two points on the psychrometric chart can be used to represent the condition of the air entering the equipment and the condition of the air leaving the equipment. The corresponding HVAC process is represented by a line which connects these two points. One point indicates the condition of the air at the beginning of the process, and the second point identifies the condition of the air after the process is completed.

Sensible or Latent Processes

There are eight possible processes (or combinations of processes) which can occur when a single stream of air flows through the HVAC equipment. Figure 2.1 indicates four of the possibilities: sensible heating, sensible cooling, latent heating (humidification) and latent cooling (dehumidification). In this figure, the initial condition of the air is described by point "A". The first four processes are identified by drawing vertical and horizontal lines through point "A". Figure 2.1 illustrates these processes.

Line A-B represents the addition of sensible heat. Since no moisture is added or removed, the temperature of the air increases, but the specific humidity remains constant. Also note that the relative humidity of the air changes because warmer air can hold more moisture than cooler air. An indirect fired furnace is a good example of the type of equipment associated with this process.

Line A-C represents the removal of sensible heat. The temperature of the air decreases and the specific humidity remains constant because no moisture is added or removed. The relative humidity changes because the potential of the cooler air to absorb and hold moisture is reduced. An air conditioner operating with a dry cooling coil is a good example of the type of equipment associated with this process.

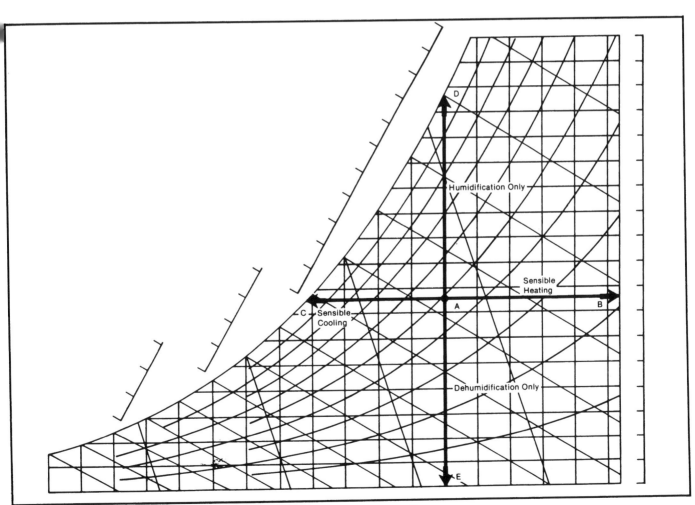

Figure 2.1 Sensible or Latent Processes

Line A-D represents a process which adds moisture to the air in such a way that the temperature of the air is unaffected. In this process, the specific humidity increases while the dry bulb temperature remains unchanged. The relative humidity increases because the air becomes more saturated with moisture. An example of the type of equipment associated with this type of process is a humidifier that uses its own source of heat to evaporate the water into the air.

Line A-E represents a process which removes moisture from the air in such a way that the temperature of the air is unaffected. In this process, the specific humidity decreases while the dry bulb temperature remains constant. The relative humidity decreases because the air becomes less saturated as moisture is removed. Liquid absorption equipment is an example of the type of equipment associated with this type of process.

Combined Sensible and Latent Processes

Figure 2.2 illustrates four additional processes which are associated with the lines that run through point A and fall within the quadrants formed by the vertical and horizontal lines described above.

Any process line located in Quadrant I represents a process which provides both heat and humidification. An example of the type of equipment associated with this process is a furnace that is equipped with a humidifier.

Any process line located in Quadrant II represents a process which provides cooling and humidification. An evaporative cooler is an example of the type of equipment associated with this process.

Any process line located in Quadrant III represents a process which provides cooling and dehumidification. An example of the type of equipment associated with this process is an air conditioner operating with a wet cooling coil.

Any process line located in Quadrant IV represents a process which provides heating and dehumidification. Absorption dehumidification equipment is an example of the type of equipment associated with this process.

Air Side Equations

Once any process line is drawn on the psychrometric chart, the sensible, latent and total loads associated with that process can be computed by using the air equations (given below) and the initial and final conditions of the air (as determined from the chart).

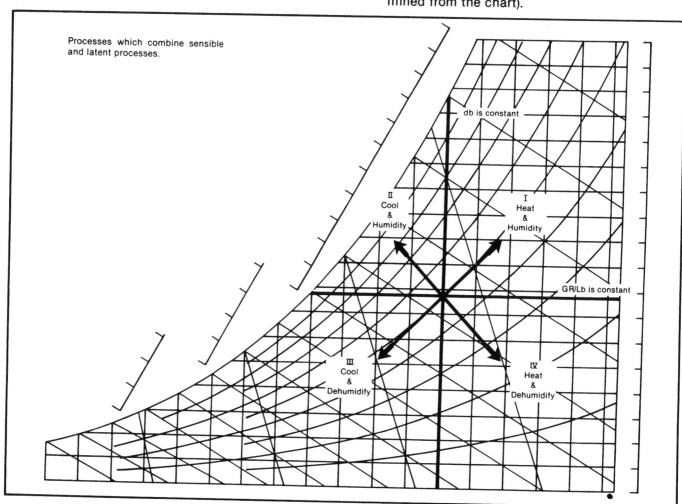

Figure 2.2 Combined Sensible and Latent Processes

The Air Side Equations Are:

$$(Qs) \text{ Sensible Load} = 1.1 \times \text{CFM} \times \text{Temperature Difference}$$
(Temperature Difference is Expressed in Degrees Fahrenheit.)

$$(Ql) \text{ Latent Load} = 0.68 \times \text{CFM} \times \text{Grains Difference}$$
(Grains Difference is Expressed in Grains Per Pound.)

$$(Qt) \text{ Total Load} = 4.45 \times \text{CFM} \times \text{Enthalpy Difference}$$
(Enthalpy Difference is Expressed in BTU Per Pound.)

Note that: $Qt = Qs + Ql$

In the equations above, the 1.1, 0.68 and 4.45 are constants which evolve when the basic laws of physics (thermodynamics) are applied to air conditioning processes.

Figure 2.3 illustrates how the sensible, latent and total loads associated with a HVAC process appear on the psychrometric chart. Note that the legs of the triangle represent the sensible and latent loads and the hypotenuse represents the total load.

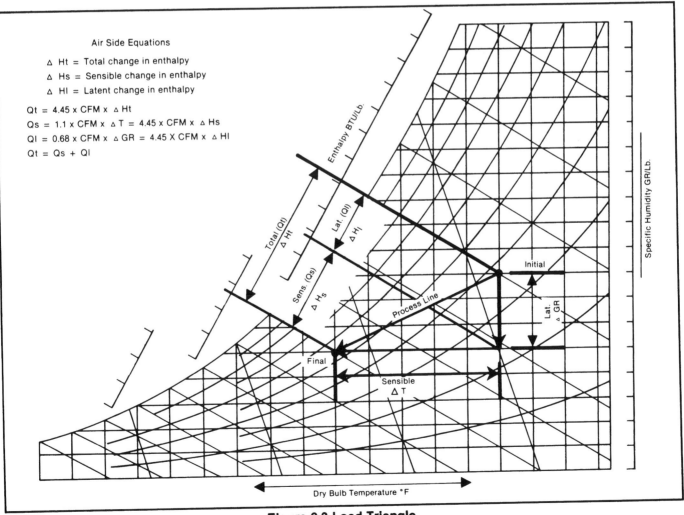

Figure 2.3 Load Triangle

19

Summary of Process Line Calculations

- A point on the chart identifies the properties of the air.

- Two points identify the properties of the air at the beginning and end of a process. The line connecting these two points is a process line.

- The process line is the hypotenuse of a right triangle. The hypotenuse of the triangle represents the total load. The legs of the triangle represent the sensible and latent loads.

- The equations used to calculate sensible, latent and total loads for a process are:

Sensible - $Qs = 1.1 \times CFM \times db$ Temperature Difference

Latent - $Ql = 0.68 \times CFM \times$ Grains Difference

Total - $Qt = 4.45 \times CFM \times$ Enthalpy Difference

Also note that when the process line is projected onto the enthalpy scale:

$Qt = 4.45 \times CFM \times$ Total Enthalpy Difference
$$(\Delta Ht)$$

$Qs = 4.45 \times CRM \times$ Sensible Enthalpy Difference
$$(\Delta Hs)$$

$Ql = 4.45 \times CFM \times$ Latent Enthalpy Difference

and

$Qt = Qs + Ql$

Examples of Psychrometric Processes

The following figures illustrate some common psychrometric processes associated with a single stream of air flowing through typical HVAC devices.

Figure 2.4 illustrates the sensible heating process. Note that the latent load is zero and that the total load equals the sensible load.

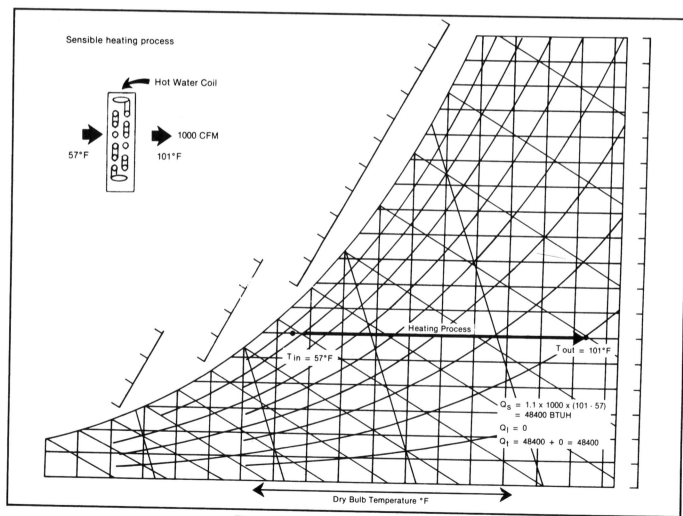

Figure 2.4 Sensible Heating Process

Figure 2.5 illustrates the pure humidification process. Note that the sensible load is zero and that the total load equals the latent load.

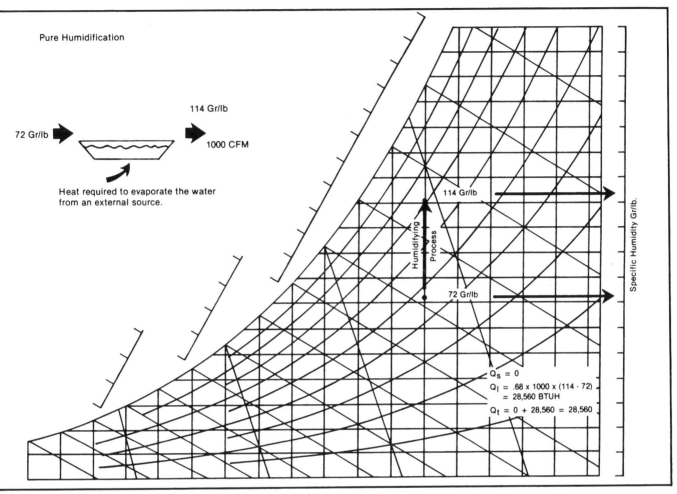

Figure 2.5 Pure Humidification Process

Figure 2.6 illustrates a cooling and dehumidification process. Note that the total load is equal to the sensible load plus the latent load and that the total load also equals (4.45 x CFM x enthalpy change).

Figure 2.7 illustrates an evaporative cooling process. Note that the total load is zero because the decrease in the sensible load is exactly offset by the increase in the latent load.

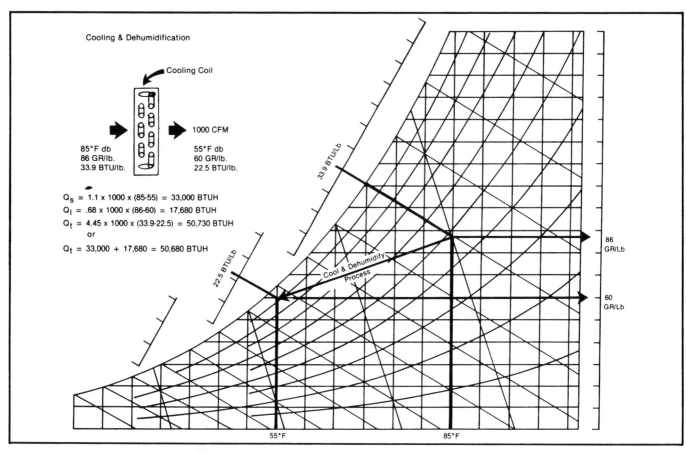

Figure 2.6 Cooling and Dehumidification Process

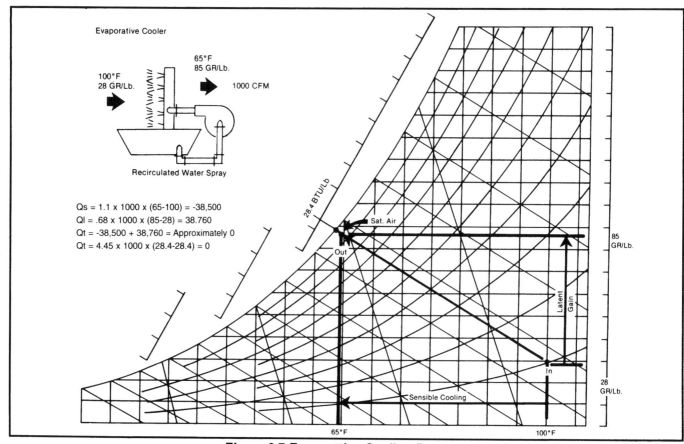

Figure 2.7 Evaporative Cooling Process

Figure 2.8 illustrates a chilled water spray cooling and dehumidification process. Note that the total load is equal to the sensible load plus the latent load and that the total load also equals (4.45 x CFM x enthalpy change).

Mixing

An additional process occurs when two separate streams of air are mixed together. For example, mixing occurs when outside air is introduced through an air handler. In this case, outdoor air is mixed with return air. Figure 2.9 shows how the psychrometric chart can be used to determine the properties of the mixed air.

The location of the condition point of the mixed air is easily determined by calculating the dry bulb temperature of the mixture.

The mixed air dry bulb temperature can be calculated by multiplying the percent of room air by the room dry bulb temperature (point B) and adding this value to the percent of outdoor air multiplied by the outdoor dry bulb temperature (point A).

Mixed db = % Room Air x Room db + % Outdoor Air x Outside db

Mixed db = % Room Air x Point B + % Outdoor Air x Point A

The mixed air condition point will fall on the intersection of the line which connects the condition points (points A & B) of the two air streams which are being mixed and the vertical line which corresponds to the dry bulb temperature of the mixed air.

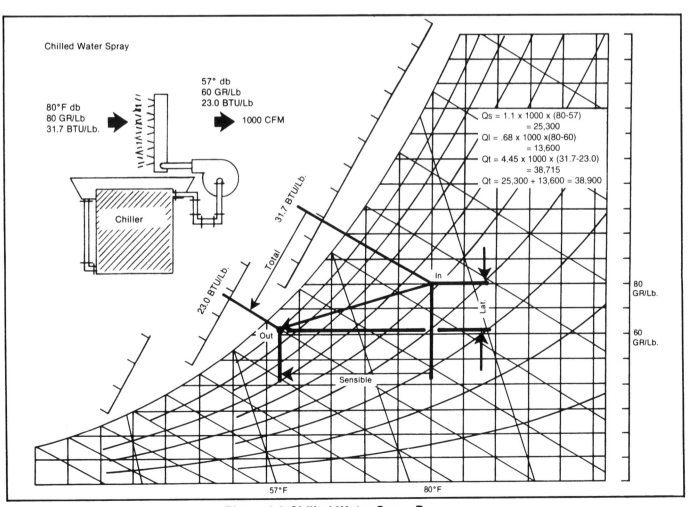

Figure 2.8 Chilled Water Spray Process

23

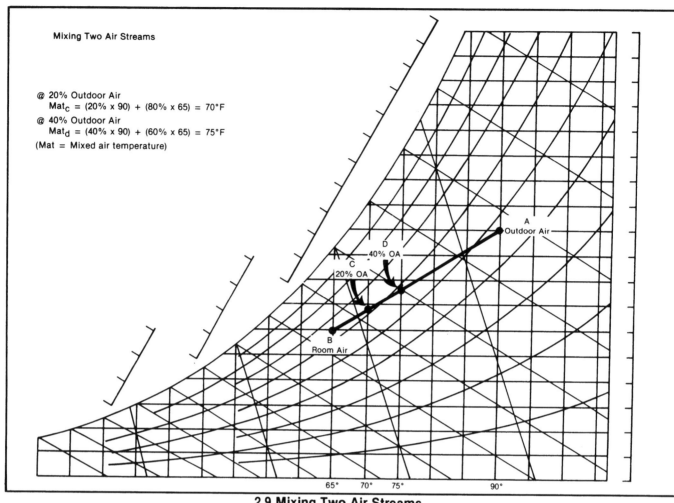

Mixing Two Air Streams

@ 20% Outdoor Air
   $Mat_c = (20\% \times 90) + (80\% \times 65) = 70°F$
@ 40% Outdoor Air
   $Mat_d = (40\% \times 90) + (60\% \times 65) = 75°F$
(Mat = Mixed air temperature)

A
Outdoor Air
D
40% OA
C
20% OA
B
Room Air

65°   70°   75°   90°

2.9 Mixing Two Air Streams

On Figure 2.9, point "A" represents a typical summer outside condition and point "B" represents the condition of the return air. If 20% outside air is mixed with 80% return air, the mixture will have the condition shown by point C. If 40% outside air is mixed with 60% return air, the mixture will have the condition shown by point "D". Note that point B represents zero percent outside air and point A represents 100% outside air.

Practice Problems
Practice Problem 2.1
2000 CFM is blown through a hot water spray (refer to Figure 2.10)

A) Draw the process line.
B) Calculate the sensible, latent and total loads.

Practice Problem 2.2
4000 CFM is blown through a cooling and dehumidifying coil (refer to Figure 2.11).

A) Draw the process line.
B) Calculate the sensible, latent and total loads.

Practice Problem 2.3
2000 CFM is cooled and dehumidified and reheated (refer to Figure 2.12).

A) Draw the process lines.
B) Calculate the cooling sensible, latent and total loads.
C) Determine the conditions of the air leaving the heating coil.

Practice Problem 2.4
3000 CFM of outdoor air at 100 db and 78 wb is mixed with 7000 CFM of return air at 70 db and 50% RH (refer to Figure 2.13).

A) Draw the process lines.
B) Determine the db temperature and specific humidity of the mixture.

Check your work. Refer to the solutions which are provided at the back of this manual.

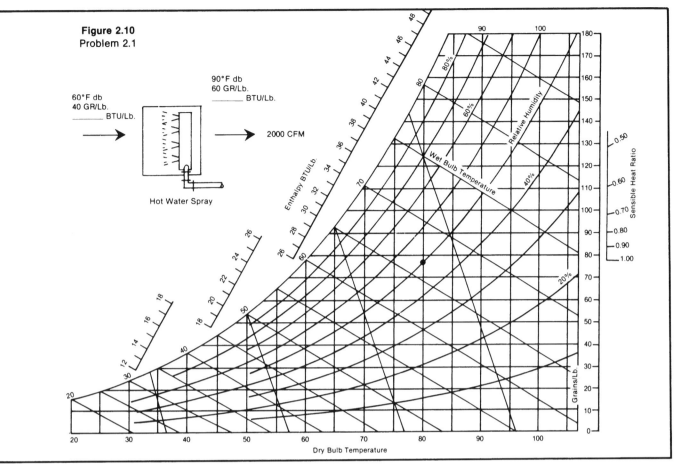

Figure 2.10
Problem 2.1

60°F db
40 GR/Lb.
_____ BTU/Lb.

90°F db
60 GR/Lb.
_____ BTU/Lb.

2000 CFM

Hot Water Spray

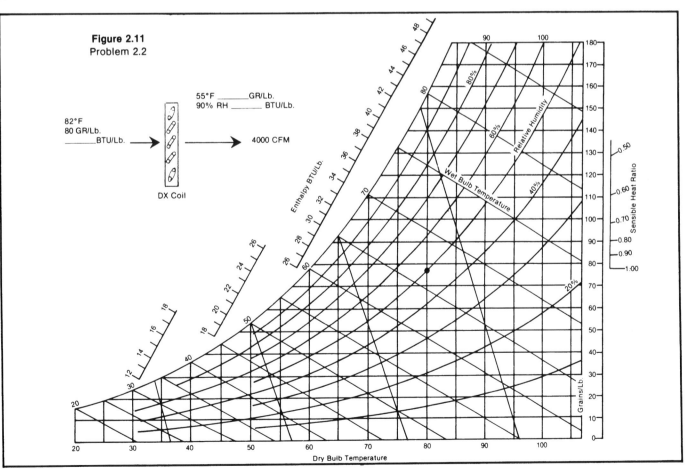

Figure 2.11
Problem 2.2

82°F
80 GR/Lb.
_____BTU/Lb.

55°F _____GR/Lb.
90% RH _____ BTU/Lb.

4000 CFM

DX Coil

25

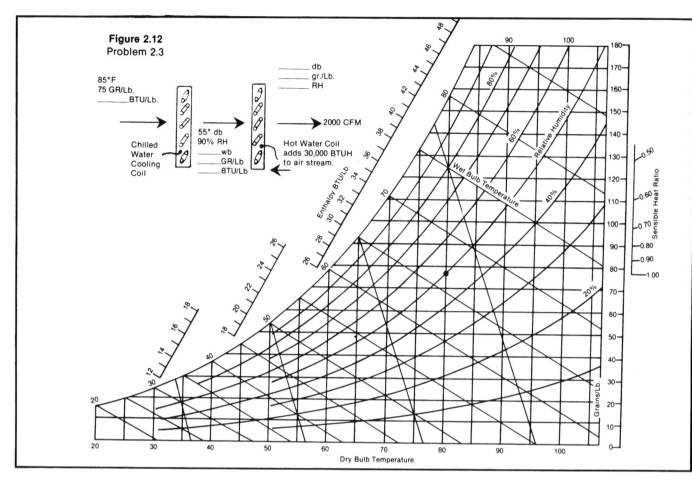

Figure 2.12
Problem 2.3

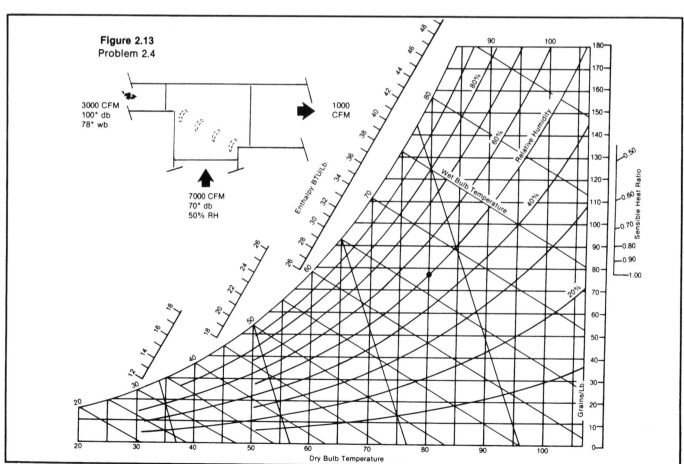

Figure 2.13
Problem 2.4

Section 3
Room Sensible Heat Ratio and Room CFM

Room Sensible Heat Ratio

The room sensible heat ratio is defined as the ratio of room (or zone) sensible heat to room (or zone) total heat. Consider the sensible heat ratios associated with the sensible and latent loads for the rooms shown below. (Each room is maintained at 75 db and 55% RH.)

Btuh	Room 1	Room 2	Room 3
Sensible	8,000	10,500	15,000
Latent	1,000	2,000	4,000

Room 1 has a RSHR (Room Sensible Heat Ratio) of:

$$8000/(8000 + 1000) = 0.89$$

Room 2 has a RSHR of:

$$10,500/12,500 = 0.84$$

Room 3 has a RSHR of:

$$15,000/19,000 = 0.79$$

The average SHR for all the rooms is:

$$(8,000 + 10,500 + 15,000)/(9,000 + 12,500 + 19,000) = 0.827$$

Room Sensible Heat Ratio Line

The room sensible heat ratio is shown on the psychrometric chart by a line which is drawn through the room condition point. Figure 3.1 shows how the room sensible heat ratio line for room 2 (RSHR = 0.84) appears on the chart.

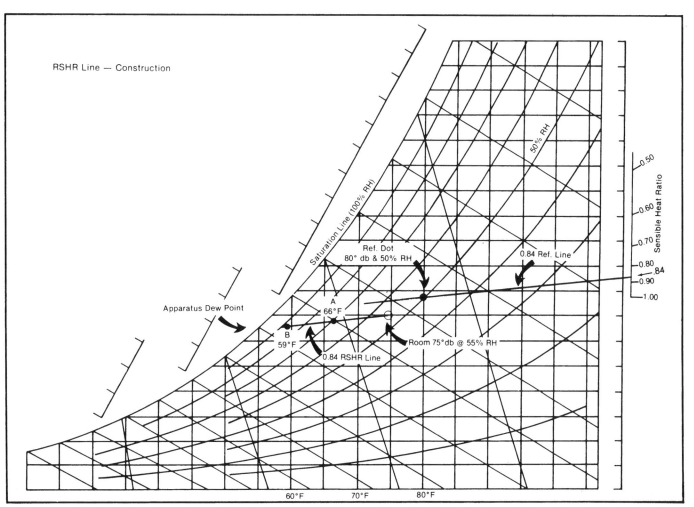

Figure 3.1 RSHR Line — Construction

Room Sensible Heat Ratio Line Construction

To draw this line:

- Locate the reference dot at 80 db and 50% RH.

- On the extreme right side of the chart locate the sensible heat factor (0.84 for this example).

- Draw a reference line from the sensible heat factor on the right side of the chart through the reference dot. (Note that all lines which are parallel to this reference line represent process lines which also have room sensible heat ratios which are equal to 0.84)

- Locate the room condition point (75 db and 55% RH in this example).

- Draw a line parallel to the reference line which passes through the room condition point.

This RSHR line can be used to determine the condition and quantity of the supply air required to maintain the desired room condition on a design day. The condition of the air supplied to the room must fall on this line. If the condition of the supply air does not fall on this line, the desired room condition will not be maintained.

Figure 3.1 indicates that points A and B are valid supply temperatures because they fall on the RSHR line. In fact, any of the points along the RSHR line that fall between the room temperature and the saturation line represent supply conditions which have the correct ratio of sensible cooling and moisture absorbing ability to maintain the design condition in a room that has RSHR of 0.84.

Design CFM (Room)

The amount of supply air (CFM) that is required to offset the room sensible and latent loads is determined by sensible heat equation and the dry bulb temperature difference between the room temperature and the supply temperature.

The room sensible heat equation is:
Room Sensible Load = 1.1 x CFM x (Room db - Supply db)

Solving for CFM:
$$CFM = \frac{Room\ Sensible\ Load}{1.1 \times (Room\ db - Supply\ db)}$$

Room 2 (as discussed above) has a RSHR of 0.84. Therefore, the line shown on Figure 3.1 is the correct RSHR line for this room. Room 2 has a sensible load of 10,500 Btuh and a latent load of 2,000 Btuh (the room is maintained at 75 db and 55% RH).

If the supply air db is 59°F (Point B, Figure 3.1), the design CFM will be:
$$CFM = \frac{10500}{1.1 \times (75-59)} = 597$$

If the supply air db is 66°F (Point A, Figure 3.1), the design CFM will be:
$$CFM = \frac{10500}{1.1 \times (75-66)} = 1061$$

Both of the air quantities calculated above will exactly offset the room sensible and the latent loads as long as the supply air condition falls on the 0.84 RSHR line. Note that the design CFM is reduced (less fan power required) when a lower supply temperature is used. However, lower supply temperatures require colder coil temperatures (increased compressor power). The supply temperature that is best for any particular application will depend on the type of cooling equipment and the type of HVAC system.

Selecting Supply Air Temperature

To select the optimum supply air temperature, the designer must consider the following:

- Packaged DX equipment can be expected to produce air temperatures leaving the coil which are 15°F to 20°F below the room temperature.

- Chilled water coils can produce air temperatures leaving the coil which are 15°F to 25°F below the room temperature.

- Larger difference between the room temperature and supply temperature will reduce the required supply CFM and save fan power.

- Lower coil temperatures will reduce the coefficient of performance (COP) of the refrigeration equipment.

- The lowest theoretical supply temperature is equal to the apparatus dew point which is located at the intersection of the RSHR line and the saturation line. In actual practice, this theoretical supply temperature will not occur because some percentage of the supply air will flow through the coil without contacting the coil surfaces. The dry bulb temperature of the resulting mixture of conditioned and bypassed air will always be higher than the apparatus dew point. Bypass factors which are associated with four, six and eight row coils will allow the relative humidity of the air leaving the coil to be maintained between 85% and 95%.

- In actual practice, a supply air condition which falls on the RSHR line and has a relative humidity between 85% and 95% is a good choice. But, remember that this condition only represents what is desired and the equipment (coil) performance data must be checked to verify that the equipment is capable of producing this condition.

- A supply condition that falls below the RSHR line can be used, but the room humidity will be lower than the desired design humidity.

- If a supply condition that falls above the RSHR line is used, the room humidity will be higher than the desired design humidity. Figure 3.2 shows the effects of supply conditions which do not fall on the RSHR line.

Multiple Room Sensible Heat Ratios

Note that if more than one room (or zone) is conditioned by a single central cooling coil, the coil will normally not be able to simultaneously satisfy the latent loads in all of the rooms. This occurs because the coil can only operate at a single sensible heat ratio and that particular sensible heat ratio may not be equal to any of the individual room sensible heat ratios.

Refer to the example given at the beginning of this section. If the coil is selected to match the RSHR for any one of the rooms, it will not match the RSHR required for the other rooms and the humidity in those rooms will be either higher or lower than desired. If it is not possible to satisfy the RSHR condition for all the rooms, one of the following choices must be made.

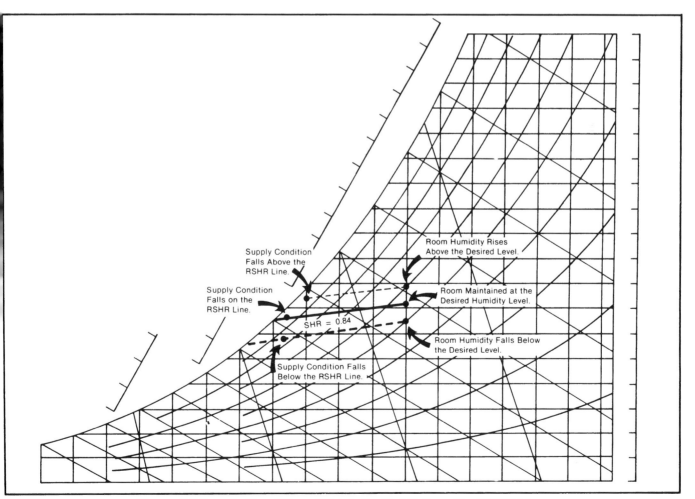

Figure 3.2 Supply Conditions Which Do Not Fall on the RSHR Line

1. If control of the room humidity in one of the rooms (or zones) is more critical than the other rooms, the RSHR for that room will establish the design sensible heat ratio and all the other rooms will have humidities that will vary from the desired design condition.

2. If none of the room humidity requirements are critical, the coil may be selected to satisfy the average humidity requirements of all of the rooms. In the example at the beginning of this section, a RSHR of 0.83 would almost satisfy Room 2. Room 1 would have a humidity lower than the design condition and Room 3 would have a humidity above the design condition. These variations are small and they are acceptable.

It is important to remember that the above discussion only applies to designs which have 100% return air and no outdoor air. The use of outside air adds an additional constraint on the procedure for determining the supply temperature off the coil. (The psychrometrics associated with selecting a coil leaving condition when the coil is operating under a ventilation load will be discussed in the next section.)

Summary

The room sensible heat ratio is defined as:

RSHR = (Room Sensible Heat)/(Room Total Heat)

- The RSHR line must be constructed so that it passes through the design room condition.

- The room design condition will be maintained if (and only if) the supply air condition falls on the room sensible heat ratio line.

- The design CFM is determined by the air side equation:

$$CFM = \frac{Room\ Sensible\ Load}{1.1\ x\ Design\ T.D.}$$

- For most situations, the relative humidity of the supply air should be selected between 85% and 95%.

- The coil performance data must be checked to verify that the selected supply air condition can actually be maintained by the equipment.

Practice Problems

3.1 A load calculation indicates that a room has a load of 7000 Btuh sensible and 800 Btuh latent. The room condition is to be maintained at 75 db and 50% rh.

A) Calculate the RSHR.

B) Draw the RSHR line on the psychrometric chart.

C) Select a supply air relative humidity condition of 90%.

D) What is the supply dry bulb temperature if the % rh of the air leaving the coil is 90%?

E) What will determine the final selection of supply dry bulb temperature?

F) Assuming the choice for item D is correct, what is the room CFM?

3.2 The building described below is to be conditioned with package roof top DX equipment. Room design is 75 db and 50% rh.

	Room No. 1		Room No. 2
Sens. Btuh =	30,000	Sens. Btuh =	18,000
Lat. Btuh =	7,000	Lat. Btuh =	5,000

	Room No. 3		Room No. 4
Sens. Btuh =	24,000	Sens. Btuh =	15,000
Lat. Btuh =	4,000	Lat. Btuh =	2,000

A) Calculate the RSHR for each space.

B) Calculate the RSHR for the entire building.

C) None of the spaces are critical - select a design RSHR for the equipment.

D) Draw the RSHR line on the psychrometric chart.

E) Select a supply condition at 85% RH off of the coil.

F) Calculate the CFM for each room.

G) Determine the room humidity in each room if the supply air to each room enters the room at the condition determined from item (E).

Check your work. Refer to the solutions provided at the back of this manual.

Section 4
Coil Sensible Heat Ratio

Coil Sensible Heat Ratio Without Ventilation
When the HVAC equipment does not include a provision for introducing outdoor air (ventilation) through the cooling coil, the room sensible heat ratio (RSHR) line completely defines all the possible supply air conditions.

In this case, the sensible and latent loads in the room and on the coil are identical and the room and the coil sensible heat ratio lines are identical. The room design condition will be maintained if the supply air condition is located anywhere on the room sensible heat ratio line.

Coil Sensible Heat Ratio With Ventilation
When outdoor air is mixed with return air before it passes through the cooling coil, the coil is subject to the room sensible and latent loads and the additional sensible and latent loads that are associated with the outdoor (ventilation) air. In this case, the ratios of sensible load to total load for the room and for the coil are usually different and the room and the coil sensible heat ratios will be different.

Figure 4.1 shows how the room and the coil sensible heat ratio lines appear on the psychrometric chart. If the design room conditions are to be maintained, the supply air condition must fall on both the room sensible heat ratio and the coil sensible heat ratio lines. In this case, there is only one possible supply condition and this occurs where the coil sensible heat ratio line crosses the room sensible heat ratio line.

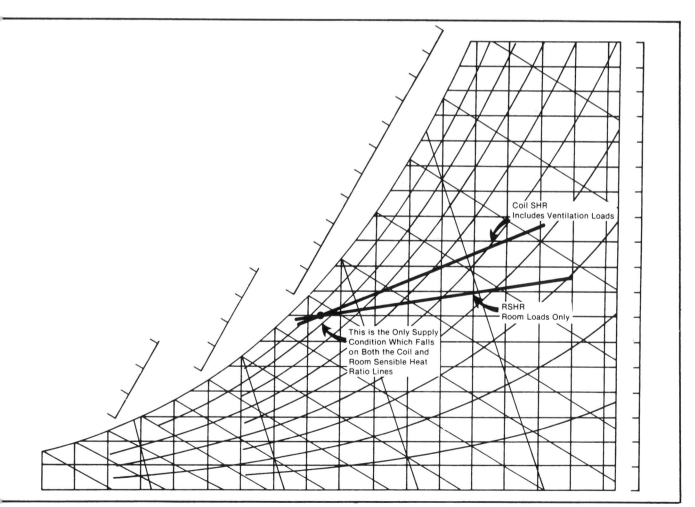

Figure 4.1 Room and Coil Sensible Heat Ratio Lines

Example - Coil Sensible Heat Ratio With Ventilation

$$RSHR = 12,000/15,000 = 0.80$$

$$CSHR = 13,500/18,500 = 0.73$$

Sensible Loads

	Btuh
Room Sensible Load =	12,000
Oat Sensible Load =	1,500
Coil Sensible Load =	13,500

Latent Loads

	Btuh
Room Latent Load =	3,000
Oat Latent Load =	2,000
Coil Latent Load =	5,000

The air leaving the coil must have the ability to cool and dehumidify the room. To do this, the supply air condition must fall on the room sensible heat ratio line.

The air leaving the coil must also be able to offset the sensible and latent loads on the coil. To do this, the supply air condition must also fall on the coil sensible heat ratio line.

The only possible supply condition which can satisfy both the room and coil loads will be located at the intersection of the two sensible heat ratio lines. Figure 4.2 shows how these lines intersect each other.

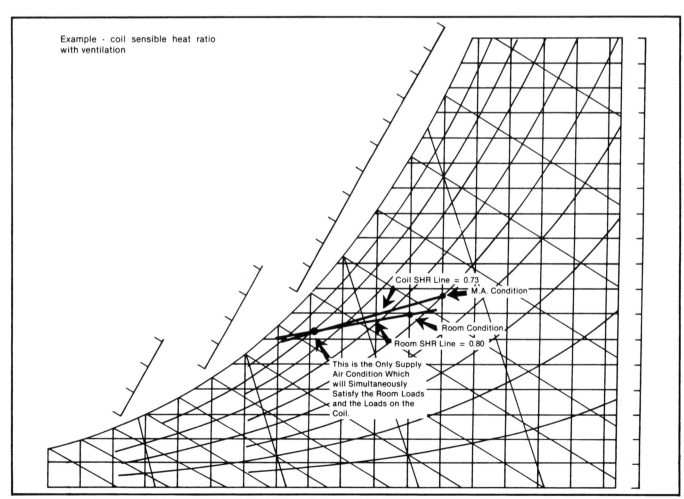

Example - coil sensible heat ratio with ventilation

Coil SHR Line = 0.73
M.A. Condition
Room Condition
Room SHR Line = 0.80
This is the Only Supply Air Condition Which will Simultaneously Satisfy the Room Loads and the Loads on the Coil.

4.2 Intersection of RSHR & CSHR Lines Denotes Supply Condition

Construction of the RSHR and CSHR Lines

It is important to understand that the room sensible heat ratio line can always be drawn on the psychrometric chart with complete certainty (refer to the previous section). This is because the room sensible heat ratio (RSHR) and the room design condition can always be determined from the load calculation information. However, this is not true for the coil sensible heat ratio line (CSHR). The following steps must be performed to draw the CSHR line.

- Locate the reference dot at 80 db and 50% RH.
- On the extreme right side of the chart locate the sensible heat factor that equals the coil sensible heat ratio.
- Draw a reference line from the sensible heat factor on the right side of the chart through the reference dot. (Note that all lines which are parallel to this reference line represent process lines which have the same sensible heat ratio.)
- Locate the mixed air condition for the air entering the coil.
- Draw a line parallel to the reference line which passes through the mixed air condition.

A trial and error solution is required because:

- The coil sensible heat ratio line cannot be drawn with complete certainty because the location of this line is determined by the mixed air condition and the coil sensible heat ratio.
- The mixed air condition and the CSHR cannot be located on the psychrometric chart without knowing the percentage of outside air.
- The percentage of outside air cannot be determined unless the supply CFM is known.
- The supply CFM depends on the dry bulb temperature difference between the room temperature and the supply temperature which depends on the intersection of the CSHR and RSHR lines.
- The coil sensible heat ratio line is not available because it is the line under construction.
- Therefore, a trial and error solution is required.
- The following example will illustrate the procedure, also refer to Figure 4.3.

Example: Construction of the coil sensible heat ratio line

Room Sensible Heat = 90,000 Btuh
Room Latent = 10,000 Btuh
RSHR = 0.90

Room Design 75 db and 50% RH
Outside Design 95 db and 75 wb

Ventilation Required = 1,000 CFM

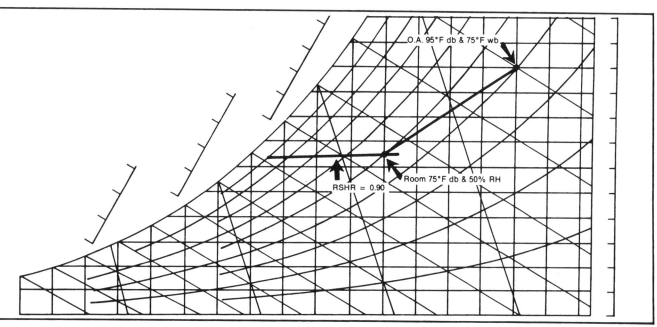

4.3 Example of Load Calculation Information

33

Note that all of the above data is available from the load calculation. Figure 4.3 shows how this data would appear on the psychrometric chart. This is the only information which is known with complete certainty. The next step is to guess at the supply condition. The following information will help in making this guess.

- The supply condition must fall on the RSHR line.
- The condition of the air leaving the cooling coil must have a db temperature and relative humidity within the normal performance range of standard cooling coils.

  * Assume water coils can provide leaving air temperatures that are between 15 and 25 degrees below the room design temperature at relative humidities between 85% and 95%.

  * Assume that DX coils installed in packaged equipment can provide leaving air temperatures which are between 15 and 20 degrees below the room temperature at relative humidities between 85% and 95%.

In the example problem outlined above, a guess for the condition of the air off the coil is required. For a packaged DX system, a leaving air db temperature of 57°F and approximately 90% RH is reasonable. Thus, the air off the coil is indicated by point A on Figure 4.4.

The coil performance calculations for the example on the preceeding page are as follows:

$$\text{Supply CFM} = \frac{RSH}{1.1 \times (75\text{-}57)} = \frac{90,000}{1.1 \times 18} = 4545 \text{ CFM}$$

$$\% \text{ Outside Air} = \frac{1000}{4545} = 22\%$$

Mixed Air Temperature = (.22 x 95) + (.78 x 75) = 79.5 db & 65.5 wb

Coil Entering Conditions = 79.5 db, & 65.5 wb

Coil Leaving Conditions = 57 db & 55.3 wb, 90% RH

Coil CFM = 4545

Total Load on the Coil = 4.45 x 4545 x (30.15 -23.35) = 137530 Btuh

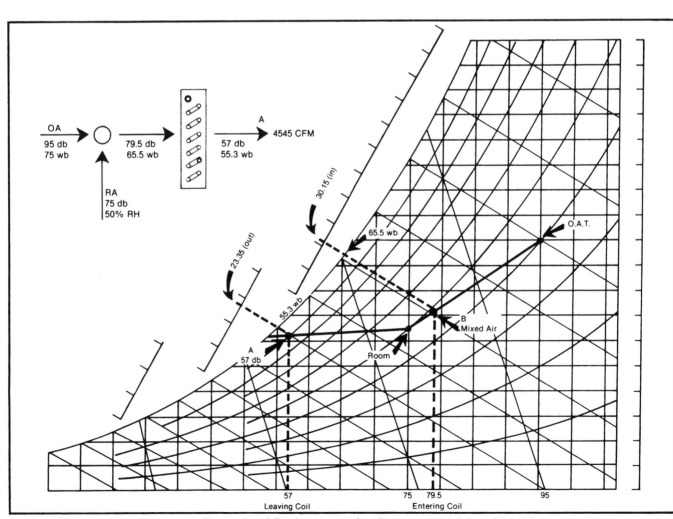

Figure 4.4 Example of Performance for Assumed Leaving Condition

Sensible Load on the Coil $= 1.1 \times 4545 \times (79.5 - 57)$
$= 112{,}489$ Btuh

Coil Sensible Heat Ratio $= \dfrac{112{,}489}{137530} = 0.818 = 0.82$

Remember that this solution represents the desired equipment (coil) performance. At this point, the manufacturer's performance data must be checked to verify that the coil is capable of providing this performance.

In this example, the manufacturer's data must show that the coil has a sensible capacity equal to (or slightly greater than) 112,489 Btuh and a total capacity equal to (or slightly greater than) 137,530 Btuh when the unit operates at 4545 CFM with an entering condition of 79.5 db and 65.5 wb and a condensing temperature of 95°F. If the coil is short on sensible or latent capacity at these conditions, the room condition will not be maintained.

Figure 4.5 shows the completed psychrometric chart. This chart is a valid solution to the example problem if, and only if, the equipment performance matches the capacities associated with the assumed coil leaving condition. (57db, 90% RH-- as shown on Figure 4.4).

Coil Bypass Factor

Also note that the required coil bypass factor can be computed from the data shown on Figure 4.5. If no air was bypassed, line C-B would represent the cooling and dehumidifying processes. The air would then leave the coil completely saturated, as indicated by point C. In actual practice, some air is bypassed so the air leaves the coil at point A.

$$BPF = \frac{LAT - ADP}{EAT - ADP} = \frac{57.0 - 53.5}{79.5 - 53.5} = 0.135$$

Where:

LAT	= Leaving Air db Temperature
ADP	= Apparatus Dew Point
EAT	= Entering Air Temperature
BPF	= Bypass Factor

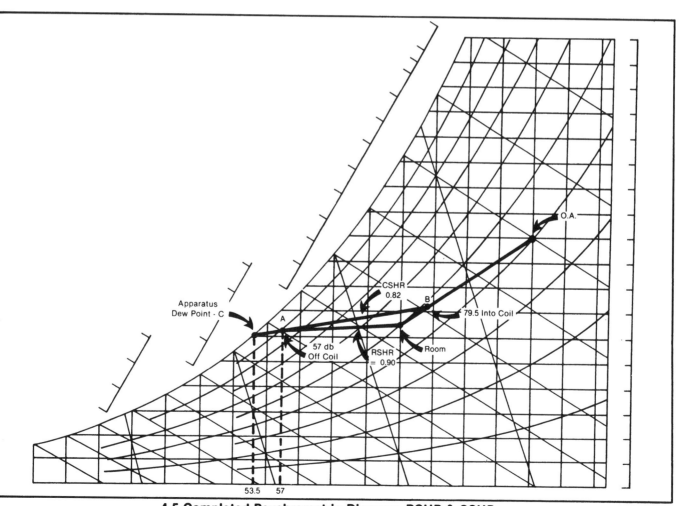

4.5 Completed Psychrometric Diagram, RSHR & CSHR

Typical Psychrometric Diagram

Figure 4.6 shows a psychrometric diagram which is typical of all cooling and dehumidifying processes which include a provision for introducing outdoor air through the equipment.

Practice Problem 4.1

Load Calculation Data:

Room Sensible Heat = 75,000 Btuh
Room Latent Heat = 11,250 Btuh
Room Summer Design = 72 db, 50% RH, 58 Grains
Outside Summer Design = 93 db, 72 wb, 84 Grains
Ventilation Required = 1,250 CFM

Assume chilled water spray equipment is used and that the leaving db temperature is 20°F below the room temperature and that the air leaves the spray at 95% RH.

Calculate:

A) Room Sensible Heat Ratio (RSHR)
B) Supply CFM
C) db Mixed Air Temperature
D) Sensible Load on the Equipment
E) Total Load on the Equipment
F) Sensible Heat Ratio for the Equipment
G) Bypass Factor

Check your work. Refer to the solution provided at the back of this manual.

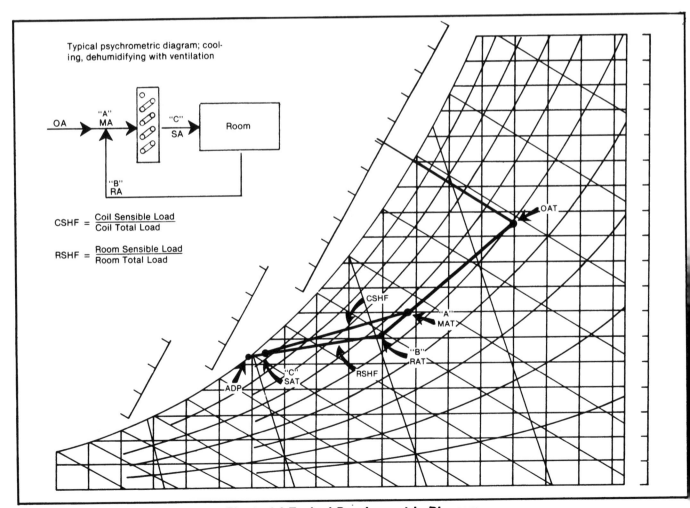

Figure 4.6 Typical Psychrometric Diagram

Section 5
Psychrometrics of HVAC Systems

The previous sections have outlined the basic psychrometric principles, the concepts of room and coil sensible heat ratios, mixing air streams, and the cooling and dehumidifying process with and without ventilation. This section will discuss the details of other psychrometric processes which usually occur in HVAC systems.

Psychrometrics for Supply Ducts and Return Air Plenums

Figure 5.1 illustrates how the sensible heat gains associated with supply ducts, return ducts or a return air plenum, appear on the psychrometric chart. The figure shows that the gain in the supply duct will increase the dry bulb temperature of supply air. The figure also shows that the sensible gain associated with the return air system will increase the return air temperature, the mixed air temperature and the coil entering air temperature.

The gains associated with supply ducts reduce the cooling capacity of the supply air because the temperature of the air that is supplied to the room is warmer than the temperature of the air off the coil. The gains that are associated with the return system increase the cooling load on the coil over and above the loads that are associated with the space and the supply duct. These gains are shown as sensible loads. The various loads associated with the psychrometric processes shown on Figure 5.1 can be computed as follows:

Assume the air handler moves 5,000 CFM.

Total sensible load on the coil; (point 1 and point 2)
$$Q = 1.1 \times 5,000 \times (80°F - 55°F) = 137,500 \text{ Btuh}$$

Total load on the coil; (point 1 and point 2)
$$Q = 4.45 \times 5,000 \times (30.5 - 22.4) = 180,225 \text{ Btuh}$$

Sensible room load; (point 3 and point 4)
$$Q = 1.1 \times 5,000 \times (75°F - 58°F) = 93,500 \text{ Btuh}$$

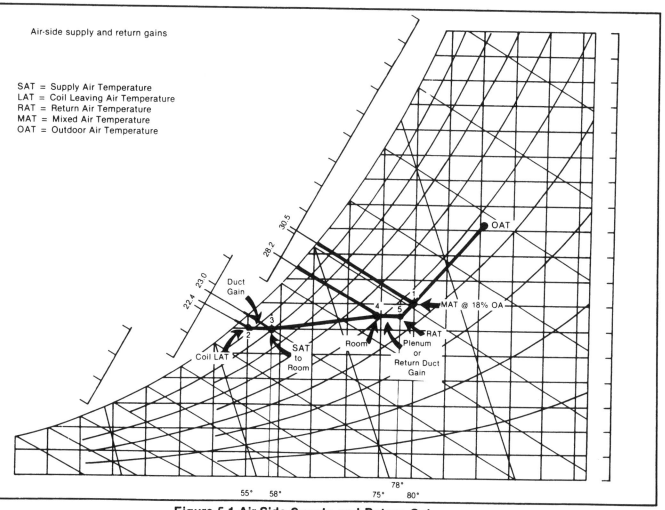

Air-side supply and return gains

SAT = Supply Air Temperature
LAT = Coil Leaving Air Temperature
RAT = Return Air Temperature
MAT = Mixed Air Temperature
OAT = Outdoor Air Temperature

Figure 5.1 Air-Side Supply and Return Gains

Total room load; (point 3 and point 4)
$Q = 4.45 \times 5{,}000 \times (28.2°F - 23°F) = 115{,}700$ Btuh

Supply duct gain; (point 2 and point 3)
$Q = 1.1 \times 5{,}000 \times (58°F - 55°F) = 16{,}500$ Btuh

Return duct gain; (point 4 and point 5)
$Q = 1.1 \times 5{,}000 \times (78°F - 75°F) = 16{,}500$ Btuh

Note: The supply and return system gains shown in the example above should not be considered to be typical. In actual practice, the duct gains (or losses) can vary considerably depending on the surrounding ambient, the amount of duct insulation, the duct size and the amount of air flowing through the duct or plenum. ACCA's Manual J and Manual N include tables which help estimate supply and return system gains and losses.

Psychrometrics for Reheat Systems

Reheat loads are shown on the psychrometric chart as sensible gains to the supply air. Figure 5.2 shows a reheat system operating during a period of reduced sensible load. At part load, the reheat system maintains the design CFM and reduces the temperature difference between the room and the supply air off of the cooling coil. This increase in supply temperature reduces the cooling capacity of the supply air just enough to match the "off design" room load. However, no reduction in latent capacity occurs. Note that the specific humidity (GR/Lb) and the potential latent capacity of the supply air remains constant as sensible heat is added to the supply air. The reheat system's ability to maintain full latent capacity at any sensible load allows the system to provide close control over both temperature and humidity in the occupied space.

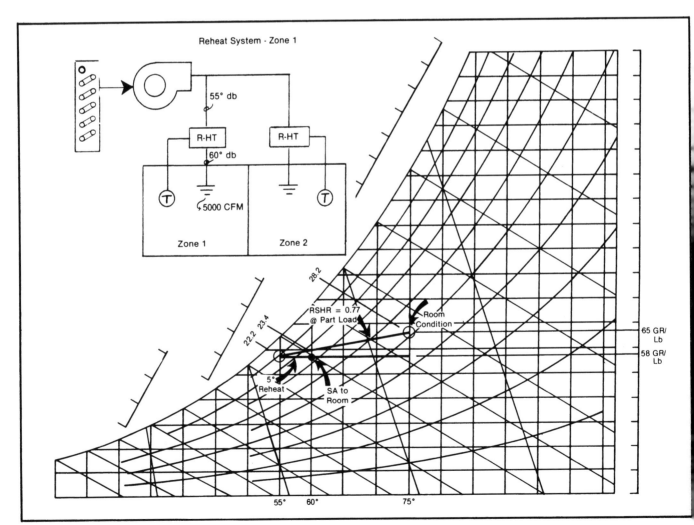

Figure 5.2 Reheat System

The various loads associated with the psychrometric processes shown on Figure 5.2 can be computed as follows:

Assume a 5,000 CFM air handler is used and the design supply temperature is 55 db & 90% RH.

Room Total Load	= 4.45 x 5,000 x (28.2 -23.4)	= 106,800 Btuh
Room Sensible Load	= 1.1 x 5,000 x (75 -60)	= 82,500 Btuh
Room Latent Load	= 0.68 x 5,000 x (65 -58)	= 23,800 Btuh
Reheat Required	= 1.1 x 5,000 x (60 -55)	= 27,500 Btuh
Total Coil Load	= 4.45 x 5,000 x (28.2 -22.2)	= 133,500 Btuh
Sensible Coil Load	= 1.1 x 5,000 x (75 -55)	= 110,000 Btuh

Note that at part load the room sensible heat ratio is (82,500/106,300) = 0.77. If the latent load remains fairly constant as the sensible load changes, the sensible heat ratio at the design sensible load (zero reheat) would be equal to (82,500 + 27,500)/(82,500 + 27,500 + 23,800) = 0.82.

In both cases, the room condition is maintained because the reheat adds just enough sensible heat to compensate for reduced sensible loads. This example also shows that reheat can be used to adjust the sensible heat ratio of the supply air so that it exactly matches the sensible heat ratio required in the conditioned space.

Variable Volume Systems

Variable volume systems cannot control humidity as closely as the reheat systems. Figure 5.3 shows the psychrometric analysis of a VAV system which is subjected to the same cooling loads as the terminal reheat system which was discussed above.

At part load, the variable volume system maintains the design supply temperature and reduces the supply CFM. The lower supply CFM reduces both the sensible and latent cooling capacity of the supply air. In the example above (terminal reheat), the part load (room sensible load) was 82,500 and the part load sensible heat ratio was 0.77. In this case, a VAV system would supply 3,750 CFM of 55°F supply air to offset the 82,500 Btuh sensible load.

Figure 5.3 shows that when the RSHR line (0.77) passes through the (55 db, 90% RH) supply condition, the room relative humidity rises to 53%. This indicates that the VAV system will not be able to maintain the 50% RH design condition at part load.

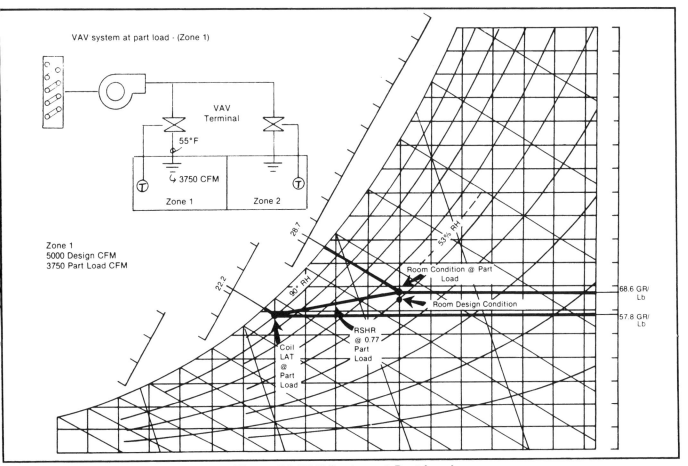

Figure 5.3 VAV System at Part Load

For 3,750 CFM the loads are:

Room Total Load   = 4.45 x 3,750 x (28.7 - 22.2)   = 108,470 Btuh

Room Sensible Load   = 1.1 x 3,750 x (75 - 55)   = 82,500 Btuh

Room Latent Load   = 0.68 x 3,750 x (68.6 - 57.8) = 27,540 Btuh

Therefore, the cooling capacity of the variable volume system exactly offsets the reduced sensible load but the room humidity drifts higher at the part load condition. However at the design load, the VAV system will supply 5,000 CFM and the room humidity will be 50% RH. The psychrometric analysis of the VAV system operating at design conditions is illustrated by Figure 5.4.

Also notice that the percentage of ventilation (outdoor air) changes as the VAV system adjusts the supply CFM to match the reduced sensible loads. Figure 5.4 shows that the VAV system supplies 1000 CFM (20% outdoor air) of ventilation air at the design conditions. At the part load condition used in the example discussed above, the supply CFM will drop to 3,750 CFM. If the minimum damper position is not adjusted for this change in supply CFM, the ventilation air quantity may drop to 750 CFM (20 percent of the part load supply CFM). Conversely, if the minimum position of the outdoor air damper is adjusted to maintain 1000 CFM of ventilation air at part load, the percentage of outdoor air entering the unit will increase to 27 percent at the design condition. Figure 5.5 illustrates the psychrometric analysis of the VAV system operation at part load with 1000 CFM of outdoor air maintained.

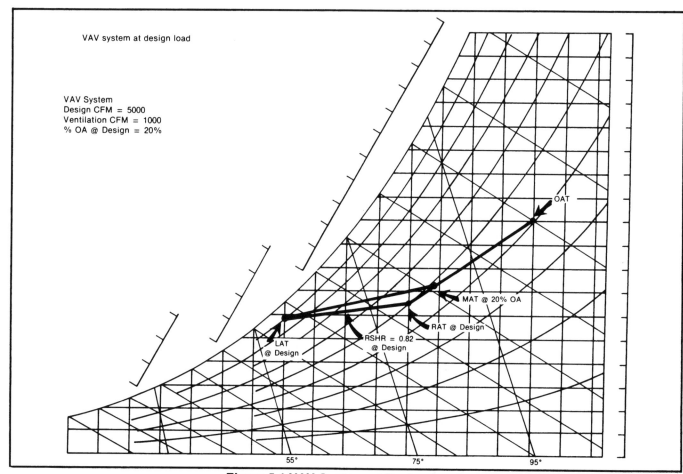

Figure 5.4 VAV System at Design Load

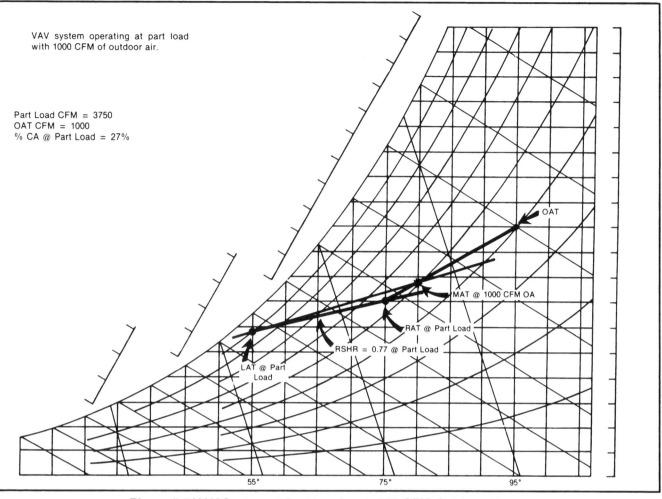

VAV system operating at part load
with 1000 CFM of outdoor air.

Part Load CFM = 3750
OAT CFM = 1000
% CA @ Part Load = 27%

OAT

MAT @ 1000 CFM OA

RAT @ Part Load

RSHR = 0.77 @ Part Load

LAT @ Part
Load

55°   75°   95°

Figure 5.5 VAV System at Part Load and 1000 CFM Outdoor Air

Multi-Zone and Dual Duct Systems

Dual duct and multi-zone systems will allow the space humidity to drift at part load conditions because, at reduced sensible loads, some of the supply air is not dehumidified when it bypasses the cooling coil. Figure 5.6 shows how the percentage of air which passes through the cooling coil is reduced at part load. In this case, the air that is supplied to the conditioned space is a mixture of dehumidified air and air which bypasses the cooling coil. The latent capacity of this mixture is reduced and the space humidity rises above the design condition.

Since dual duct and multi-zone systems are constant volume systems, the amount of ventilation air entering the unit does not vary at reduced loads.

Evaporative Cooling

Figure 5.7 shows how an evaporative cooling system would appear on the psychrometric chart. Notice that the wet bulb temperature of the air is constant as the evaporative cooling process occurs. Figure 5.7 shows that as the air is cooled by the spray, its specific humidity increases, the dry bulb temperature decreases, and the wet bulb temperature remains constant. In this case, the reduction in the sensible heat content of the supply air is exactly equal to the gain in latent heat and the total heat contained in the air stream does not change.

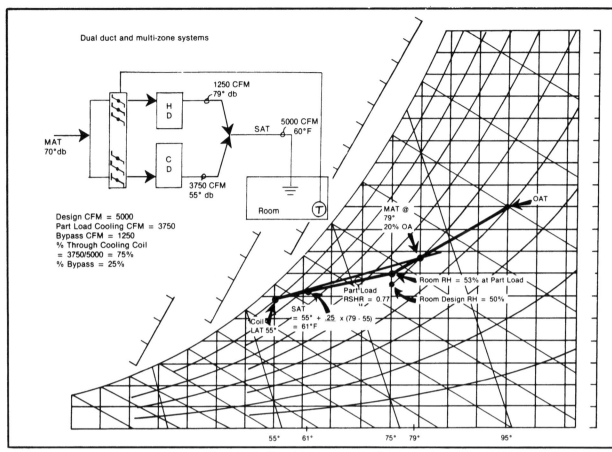

Figure 5.6 Dual Duct and Multi-Zone Systems

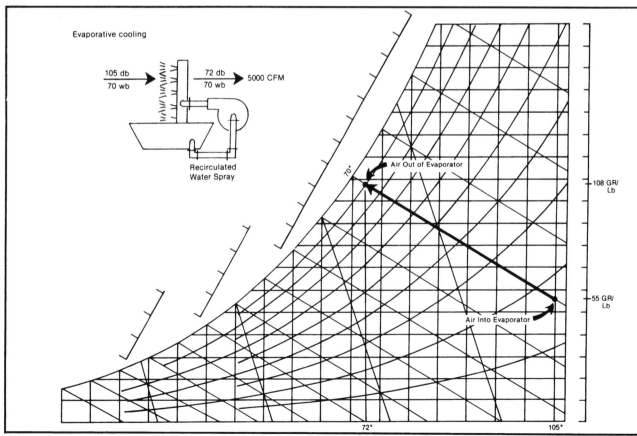

Figure 5.7 Evaporative Cooling

For 5,000 CFM the loads are:

Reduction in sensible heat
= 1.1 x 5,000 x (105-72) = 181,000 Btuh

Gain in latent heat
= 0.68 x 5,000 x (108-55) = 181,000 Btuh

Change in total heat = 0

In arid areas, the evaporator can be used to maintain comfort conditions in the occupied space. Figure 5.8 shows the psychrometrics for evaporative cooling as applied to a small commercial building. In this case, 5,000 CFM of outside air is processed by the evaporative cooler. The air enters the cooler at 100°F db and 13% RH and leaves at 65.5°db and 90% RH. (Note that the air will not leave the cooler completely saturated because some air bypasses the water spray.) The

65.5°F db supply air is then able to cool the space. If the space db is maintained at 80°F, the evaporative cooler will provide 79,750 Btuh (1.1 x 5,000 (80 - 65.5)) of sensible cooling to the space.

Note that the evaporative process is only effective for comfort cooling if a source of relatively dry air is available.

Figure 5.9 shows what would happen if evaporative cooling is used in a slightly more humid climate. In this case, the outside air temperature remains at 100°F db, but the outdoor relative humidity is increased to 22%. Notice that if the sensible load in the occupied space remains at 79,850 Btuh, the room condition rises to 85.5°F db and 55% RH.

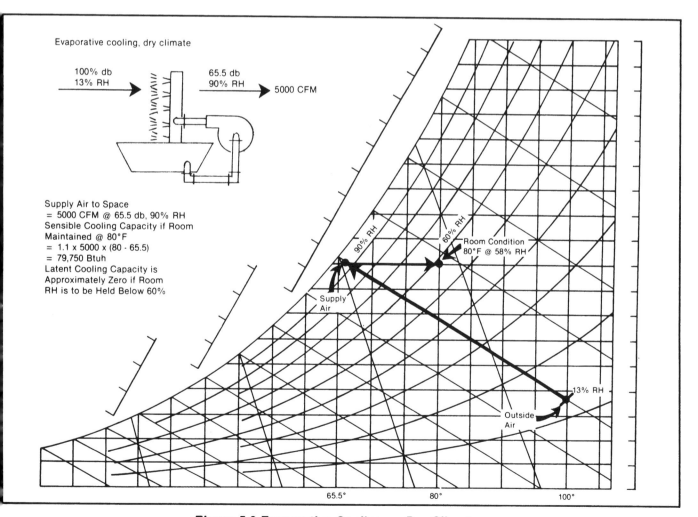

Figure 5.8 Evaporative Cooling — Dry Climate

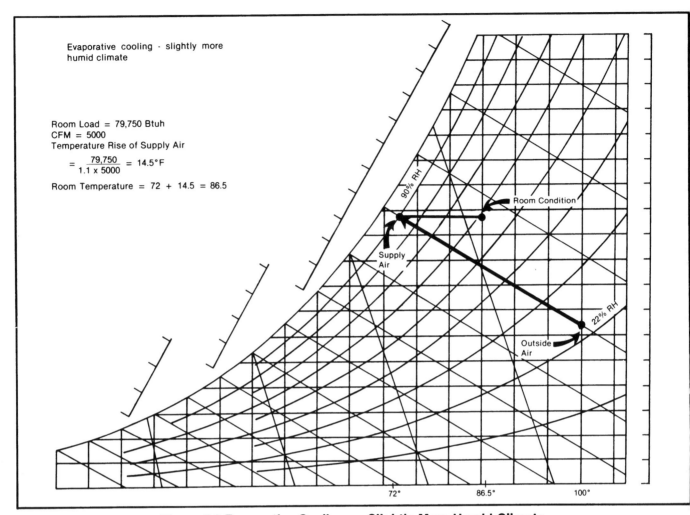

Evaporative cooling - slightly more humid climate

Room Load = 79,750 Btuh
CFM = 5000
Temperature Rise of Supply Air

$$= \frac{79,750}{1.1 \times 5000} = 14.5°F$$

Room Temperature = 72 + 14.5 = 86.5

90% RH

Room Condition

Supply Air

22% RH

Outside Air

72°   86.5°   100°

Figure 5.9 Evaporative Cooling — Slightly More Humid Climate

SOLUTIONS
TO
PRACTICE PROBLEMS

Solutions

Solutions — Section 1

1.1 58.0°F, 48.3%, 13.5 cu. ft./lb, 52.6 GR/Lb, 49.0°F

1.2 94.1°F, 41.56%, 14.3 cu. ft/lb, 38.34 BTU/Lb, 67.0°F

1.3 100%, 13.34 cu. ft./lb, 26.41 BTU/Lb, 77.3 GR/Lb, 60.0°F

SECTION 2

2.1 — Refer to Figure 2.14 Below
Solution to Practice Problem 2.1

$Qs = 1.1 \times 2000 \times (90-60) = 66000$ Btuh
$Ql = .68 \times 2000 \times (60-40) = 27200$ Btuh
$Qt = 4.45 \times 2000 \times (31.2-20.6) = 94340$ Btuh
OR
$Qt = 6600 + 27200 = 93200$ Btuh

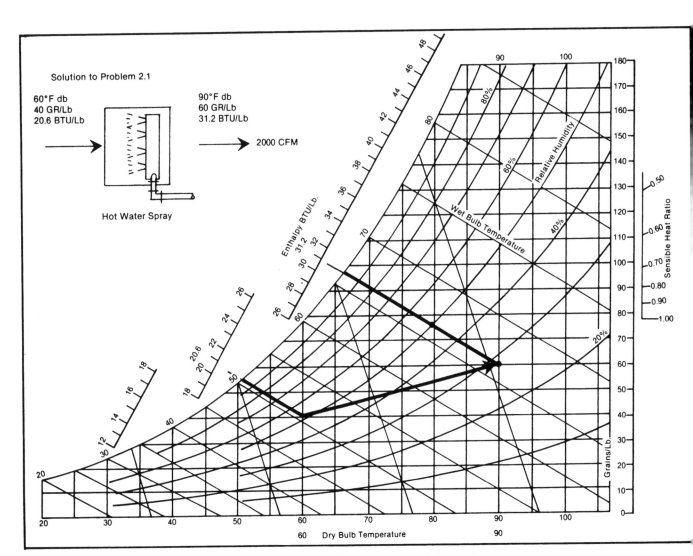

Figure 2.14 — Solution to Problem 2.1

Solutions

SECTION 2 (CONTINUED)

2.2 — Refer to Figure 2.15 Below
Solution to Practice Problem 2.2

Qs = 1.1 x 4000 x (82-55) = 118,800 Btuh
Ql = .68 x 4000 x (80-58) = 59,840 Btuh
Qt = 4.45 x 4000 x (32.4-22.2) = 181,560
QR
Qt = 118,800 + 59,840 Btuh

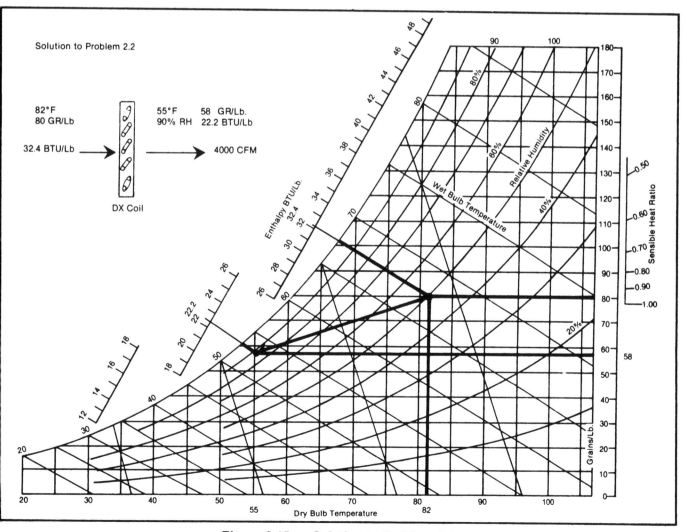

Figure 2.15 — Solution to Problem 2.2

Solutions

SECTION 2 (CONTINUED)

2.3 Refer to Figure 2.16 Below
Solution to Practice Problem 2.3

Qs = 1.1 x 2000 x (85-55) = 66,000 Btuh
Ql = .68 x 2000 x (75-58) = 23,120 Btuh
Qt = 4.45 x 2000 x (32.4-22.2) = 90,780 Btuh
QR
Qt = 66,000 + 23,120 = 89,120 Btuh

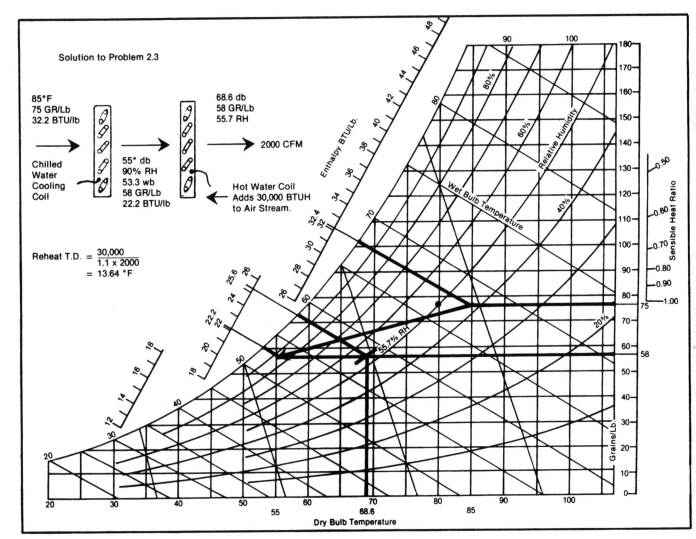

Figure 2.16 — Solution to Problem 2.3

Solutions

2.4 Refer to Figure 2.17 Below
Solution to Practice Problem 2.4

db = 79
GR = 70.9

MAT = (100 db x 30%) + (70 db x 70%)
   = 30 + 49 = 79 db

NOTE: As you work these problems you may have noticed that:

Qs = 1.1 x CFM x TD
          +
QI = .68 x CFM x $^\wedge$ GR

Does not exactly equal the value for

Qt = 4.45 x CFM x $^\wedge$ H

This occurs because the constants 1.1, 0.68 and 4.45 are only approximations and this introduces some error in the calculation. Do not worry about this small discrepancy either:

Qt = Qs + QI
or
Qt = 4.45 x CFM x Enthalpy Difference
will be acceptable answers.

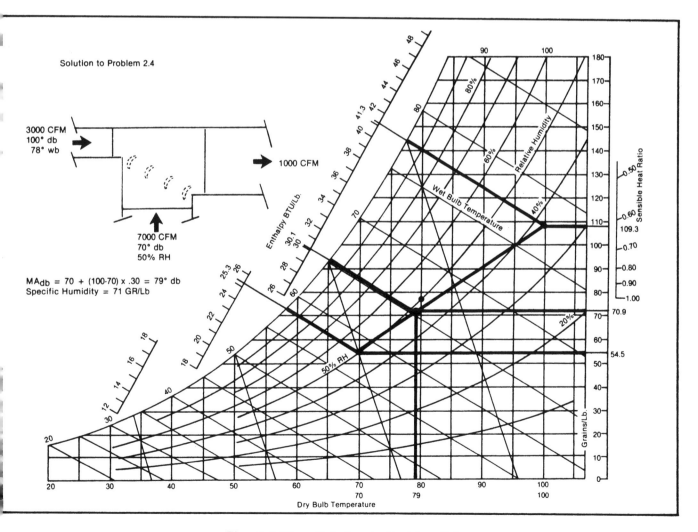

Figure 2.17 — Solution to Problem 2.4

Solutions

SECTION 3

Solution to Problem 3.1

Refer to Figure 3.3

A) 7000/78000 = 0.897 round to 0.90

B) See Figure 3.3

C) Assume 90% RH

D) db = 56.5 F, wb = 54.5°F

E) Manufacturers data on coil performance

F) Room CFM = $\dfrac{7000}{1.1 \times (75-56.5)}$ = 344 CFM

Solution to Problem 3.2

Refer to Figures 3.4 and 3.5

A) RM.1 = 0.81, RM 2 = 0.78, RM 3 = 0.86, RM 4 = 0.88

B) 0.83 (Rounded)

C) 0.83 is good. It lies midway between the extremes and it will meet the sensible and latent requirements of the entire building.

D) See Figure 3.4

E) 18°F below room temperature is normal for packaged equipment, therefore the SAT = 57 db.

F) RM 1 = 1515, RM 2 = 909, RM 3 = 1212, RM 4 = 758

G) See Figure 3.5. The room conditions can be determined by constructing RSHR lines so that they pass through the supply condition. All the rooms will be maintained at 75 db because the CFM supplied to each room was correctly determined from the room sensible load, However, the room relative humidities will vary because the design RSHR of 0.83 does not match any of the actual room RSHR's. Figure 3.5 shows that the deviation in room humidities is only a few percentage points from the desired condition of 75 db and 50% RH.

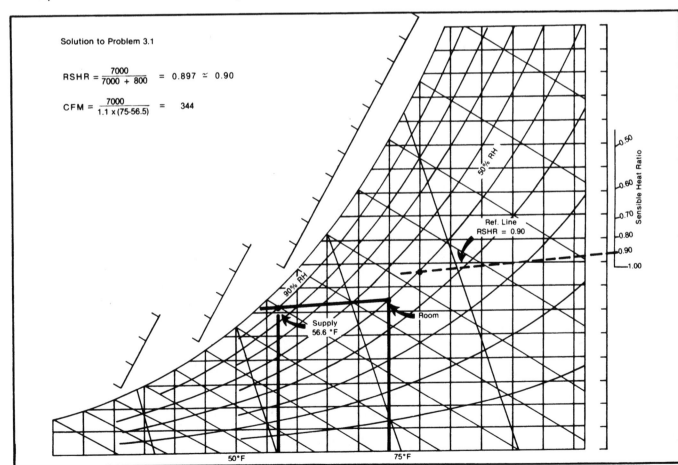

Figure 3.3 — Solution to Problem 3.1

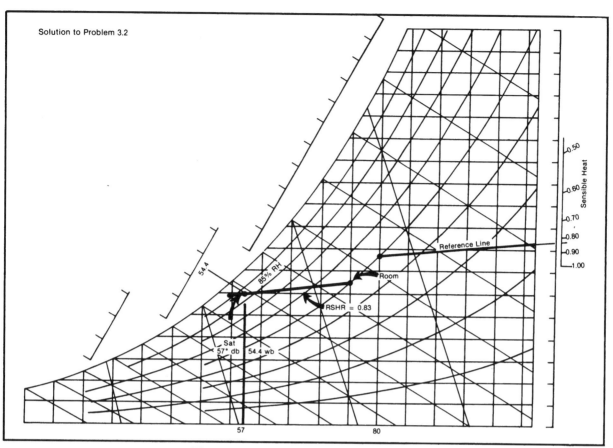

Figure 3.4 — Solution to Problem 3.2

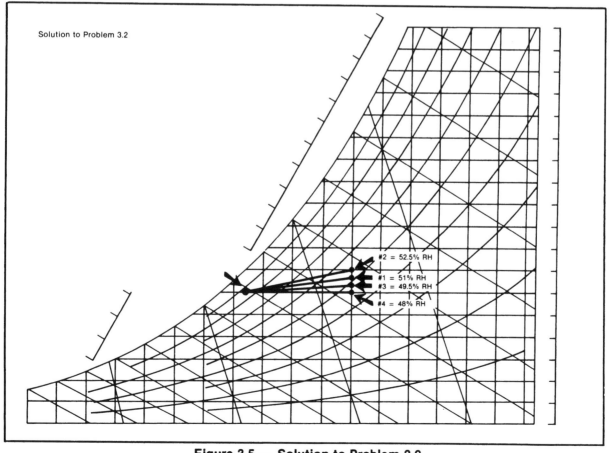

Figure 3.5 — Solution to Problem 3.2

Solutions

Solution for Practice Problem 4.1

Figure 4.7 illustrates the completed psychrometric diagram and the calculations required to determine the various parameters are as follows:

Room @ 72 db, 50% RH, 58 GR, 26.45 Btu/Lb
OA @ 93 d, 72 wb, 84 GR, 33.85 Btu/Lb

$$RSHR = \frac{75000}{75000 + 11250} = 0.87$$

$$CFM = \frac{75000}{1.1 \times (72\text{-}52)} = 3409$$

% OA = 1250/3409 = 36.7%

MAT = (93 x .37) + (72 x .63) = 79.7 F
    = 79.7 db, 64.5 wb, 67 GR, 29.7 Btu/Lb

Sens. Coil Load = 1.1 x 3409 x (79.7-52) = 103871

Total Coil Load = 4.45 x 3409 x (29.7-20.85) = 134255

Coil SHR = 103872/134254 = 0.774

$$Coil\ BF = \frac{52.49}{79.7\text{-}49} = 0.098$$

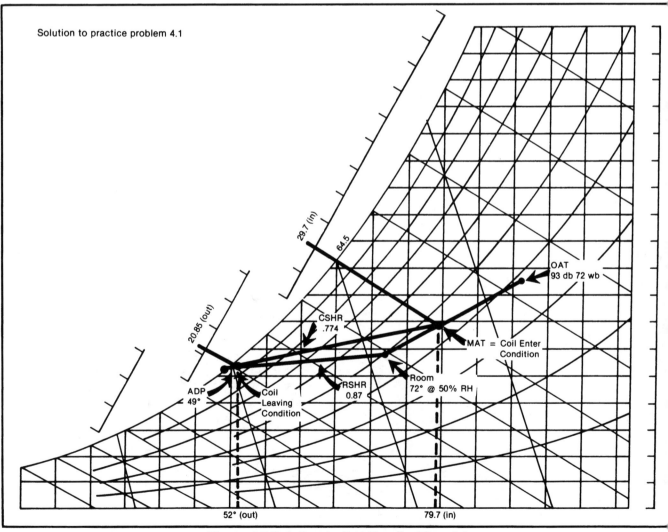

Figure 4.7 Solution to Practice Problem 4.1

INDEX